Patterning Techniques

A pattern is a repetition of shapes and lines that can be simple or complex depending on your preference and the space you want to fill. Even complicated patterns start out very simple with either a line or a shape.

Repeating shapes (floating)

Shapes and lines are the basic building blocks of patterns. Here are some example shapes that we can easily turn into patterns:

Before we turn these shapes into patterns, let's spruce them up a bit by outlining, double-stroking (going over a line more than once to make it thicker), and adding shapes to the inside and outside.

To create a pattern from these embellished shapes, all you have to do is repeat them, as shown below. You can also add small shapes in between the embellished shapes, as shown.

These are called "floating" patterns because they are not attached to a line (like the ones described in the next example). These floating patterns can be used to fill space anywhere and can be made big or small, short or long, to suit your needs.

Tip

Draw your patterns in pencil first, and then go over them with black or color. Or draw them with black ink and color them afterward. Or draw them in color right from the start. Experiment with all three ways and see which works best for you!

Tip

If you add shapes and patterns to these coloring pages using pens or markers, make sure the ink is completely dry before you color on top of them; otherwise, the ink may smear.

Repeating shapes (attached to a line)

Start with a line, and then draw simple repeating shapes along the line. Next, embellish each shape by outlining, double-stroking, and adding shapes to the inside and outside. Check out the example below.

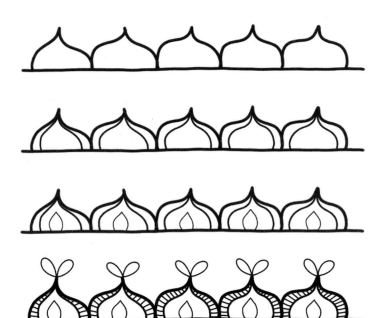

You can also draw shapes in between a pair of lines, like this:

Embellishing a decorative line

You can also create patterns by starting off with a simple decorative line, such as a loopy line or a wavy line, and then adding more details. Here are some examples of decorative lines:

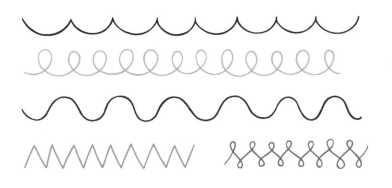

Color repetition

Patterns can also be made by repeating sets of colors. Create dynamic effects by alternating the colors of the shapes in a pattern so that the colors themselves form a pattern.

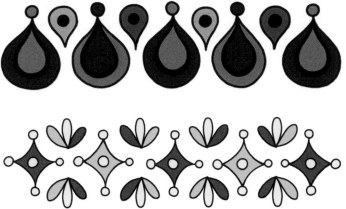

Next, embellish the line by outlining, double-stroking, and adding shapes above and below the line as shown here:

Tip

Patterns don't have to follow a straight line—they can curve, zigzag, loop, or go in any direction you want! You can draw patterns on curved lines, with the shapes following the flow of the line above or below.

These types of patterns look great when attached to the inner or outer edge of a drawing, such as the inside of a flower petal or butterfly wing.

Coloring Techniques & Media

My favorite way to color is to combine a variety of media so I can benefit from the best that each has to offer. When experimenting with new combinations of media, I strongly recommend testing first by layering the colors and media on scrap paper to find out what works and what doesn't. It's a good idea to do all your testing in a sketchbook and label the colors/brands you used for future reference.

Markers & colored pencils

Smooth out areas colored with marker by going over them with colored pencils. Start by coloring lightly, and then apply more pressure if needed.

marker   +   colored pencil   =   smoother result

Test your colors on scrap paper first to make sure they match. You don't have to match the colors if you don't want to, though. See the cool effects you can achieve by layering a different color on top of the marker below.

Markers (horizontal) overlapped with colored pencils (vertical).

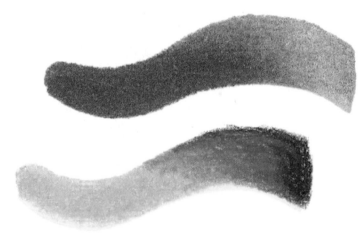

Purple marker overlapped with white and light blue colored pencils. Yellow marker overlapped with orange and red colored pencils.

Markers & gel pens

Markers and gel pens go hand in hand, because markers can fill large spaces quickly, while gel pens have fine points for adding fun details.

White gel pens are especially fun for drawing over dark colors, while glittery gel pens are great for adding sparkly accents.

Shading

Shading is a great way to add depth and sophistication to a drawing. Even layering just one color on top of another color can be enough to indicate shading. And of course, you can combine different media to create shading.

Colored with markers; shading added to the inner corners of each petal with colored pencils to create a sense of overlapping.

Colored and shaded with colored pencils.

Lines and dots were added with black ink to indicate shading and then colored over with markers.

Color Theory

Check out this nifty color wheel. Each color is labeled with a P (primary), S (secondary), or T (tertiary). The **primary colors** are red, yellow, and blue. They are "primary" because they can't be created by mixing other colors. Mixing primary colors creates the **secondary colors** orange, green, and purple (violet). Mixing a primary color and a secondary color together creates the **tertiary colors** yellow-orange, yellow-green, blue-green, blue-purple, red-purple, and red-orange.

Working toward the center of the six large petals, you'll see three rows of lighter colors, called tints. A **tint** is a color plus white. Moving in from the tints, you'll see three rows of darker colors, called shades. A **shade** is a color plus black.

The colors on the top half of the color wheel are considered **warm** colors (red, yellow, orange), and the colors on the bottom half are called **cool** (green, blue, purple).

Colors opposite one another on the color wheel are called **complementary**, and colors that are next to each other are called **analogous**.

Look at the examples and note how each color combo affects the overall appearance and "feel" of the butterfly. For more inspiration, check out the colored examples on the following pages. Refer to the swatches at the bottom of the page to see the colors selected for each piece.

Warm colors

Cool colors

Warm colors with cool accents

Cool colors with warm accents

Tints and shades of red

Tints and shades of blue

Analogous colors

Complementary colors

Split complementary colors

Happiness is a butterfly, which when pursued, is always just beyond your grasp, but which, if you will sit down quietly, may alight upon you.

—Nathaniel Hawthorne

I have a room all to myself; it is nature.

—Henry David Thoreau

Turn your face to the sun and
the shadows will fall behind you.

—Maori proverb

May the wings of the butterfly kiss the sun
And find your shoulder to light on,
To bring you luck, happiness and riches
Today, tomorrow and beyond.

—Irish blessing

Be happy for this moment.
This moment is your life.

—Omar Khayyam

Every great dream begins with a dreamer.
Always remember, you have within you the strength,
the patience, and the passion
to reach for the stars to change the world.

—Harriet Tubman

Where flowers bloom, so does hope.

—Lady Bird Johnson

A seed hidden in the heart of an apple
is an orchard invisible.

—Welsh proverb

_____
_____
_____
_____
_____
_____
_____
_____
_____
_____

Earth laughs in flowers.

—Ralph Waldo Emerson

Any glimpse into the life of an animal
quickens our own and makes it so much
the larger and better in every way.

—John Muir

Till my soul is full of longing
For the secret of the sea,
And the heart of the great ocean
Sends a thrilling pulse through me.

—Henry Wadsworth Longfellow, "The Secret of the Sea"

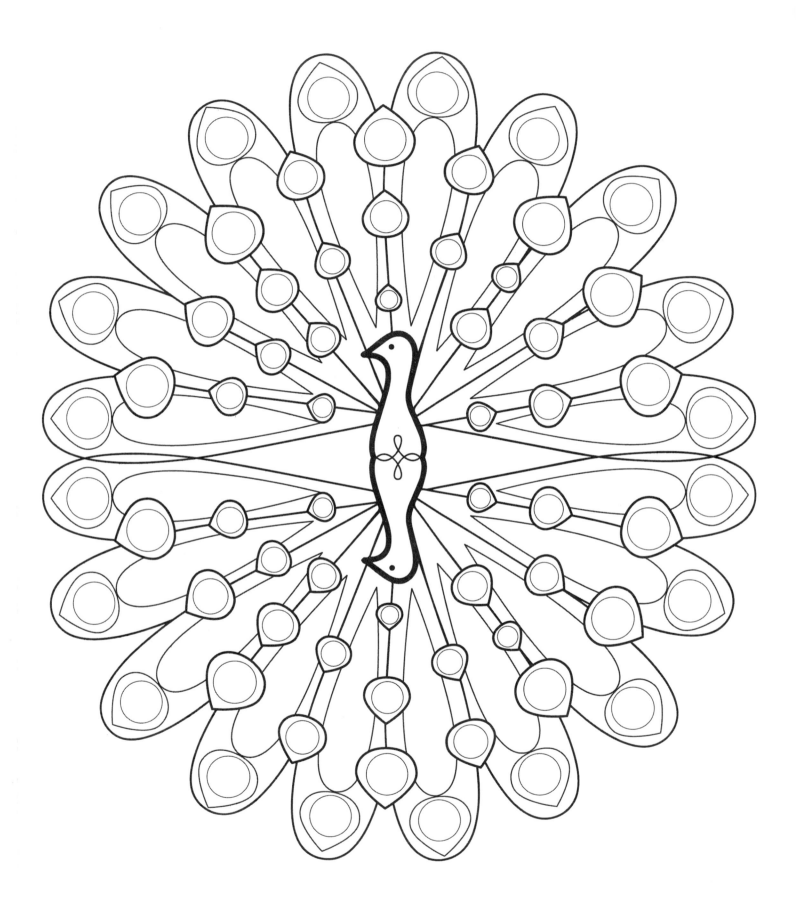

Those who dwell among the beauties and mysteries
of the earth are never alone or weary of life.

—Rachel Carson

In all things of nature there is
something of the marvelous.

—Aristotle

A bird doesn't sing because he has an answer.
He sings because he has a song.

—Joan Walsh Anglund

Be like the bird, who
Halting in his flight
On limb too slight,
Feels it give way beneath him,
Yet sings
Knowing he hath wings.

—Victor Hugo, "The Bird"

Those who contemplate the beauty of the Earth
find reserves of strength that will endure
as long as life lasts.

—Rachel Carson

If you want something you've never had,
then you've got to do something you've never done.

—Unknown

I believe that there is a subtle magnetism in Nature,
which, if we unconsciously yield to it, will direct us aright.

—Henry David Thoreau

The ocean stirs the heart, inspires the imagination, and brings eternal joy to the soul.

—Wyland

Go out, go out I beg of you
And taste the beauty of the wild.
Behold the miracle of the earth
With all the wonder of a child.

—Edna Jaques

_____

_____

_____

_____

_____

_____

_____

_____

_____

_____

And this, our life, exempt from public haunt,
finds tongues in trees, books in the running brooks,
sermons in stones, and good in everything.

—William Shakespeare

Now I see the secret of the making of the best persons:
It is to grow in the open air and
to eat and sleep with the earth.

—Walt Whitman

The indescribable innocence of and beneficence of Nature—
of sun and wind and rain, of summer and winter
—such health, such cheer, they afford forever!

—Henry David Thoreau

Just living is not enough…
one must have sunshine, freedom,
and a little flower.

—Hans Christian Andersen

The cure for anything is salt water—
sweat, tears, or the sea.

—Isak Dinesen

Nature never hurries.
Atom by atom, little by little
she achieves her work.

—Ralph Waldo Emerson

The poetry of the earth is never dead.

—John Keats

I go to nature to be soothed and healed,
and to have my senses put in order.

—John Burroughs

Forget not that the earth delights to feel your bare feet
and the winds long to play with your hair.

—Kahlil Gibran

Keep your faith in all beautiful things.
In the sun when it is hidden.
In the spring when it is gone.

—Roy Rolfe Gilson